# The Paideia Pr

# THE PAIDEIA PROPOSAL

## An Educational Manifesto

### MORTIMER J. ADLER

*ON BEHALF OF THE MEMBERS OF THE PAIDEIA GROUP*

COLLIER BOOKS
*Macmillan Publishing Company*
New York
COLLIER MACMILLAN PUBLISHERS
London

Macmillan Publishing Company
866 Third Avenue, New York, N.Y. 10022
Collier Macmillan Canada, Inc.

---

Library of Congress Cataloging in Publication Data

Adler, Mortimer Jerome, 1902–
    The Paideia proposal.

    1. Education—United States—Aims and objectives.
2. Educational equalization—United States.   3. Education—Philosophy.   I. Title.
LA210.A534      370′.973      82-7169
ISBN 0-02-064100-1           AACR2

---

First Paperback Edition 1982

20   19   18   17   16   15   14   13

Printed in the United States of America

*The Paideia Proposal* is also published in a
hardcover edition by Macmillan Publishing Company

Macmillan books are available at special discounts for bulk purchases for sales promotions, premiums, fundraising, or educational use. For details, contact:

Special Sales Director
Macmillan Publishing Company
866 Third Avenue
New York, N.Y. 10022

The Paideia Group wishes to express its gratitude to the John D. and Catherine T. MacArthur Foundation for financial support needed to carry on the opening stages of its work.

---

P A I D E I A (py-dee-a) from the Greek *pais, paidos:*
the upbringing of a child. (Related to pedagogy and
pediatrics.) In an extended sense, the equivalent of
the Latin *humanitas* (from which "the humanities"),
signifying the general learning that should be the
possession of all human beings.

# Members of the Paideia Group

MORTIMER J. ADLER, *Chairman*
Director, Institute for Philosophical Research;
Chairman, Board of Editors, Encyclopaedia Britannica

JACQUES BARZUN, former Provost, Columbia University; Literary Adviser, Charles Scribner's Sons

OTTO BIRD, former head, General Program of Liberal Studies, University of Notre Dame

LEON BOTSTEIN, President, Bard College; President, Simon's Rock of Bard College

ERNEST L. BOYER, President, The Carnegie Foundation for the Advancement of Teaching, Washington, D.C.

NICHOLAS L. CAPUTI, Principal, Skyline High School, Oakland, California

DOUGLASS CATER, Senior Fellow, Aspen Institute for Humanistic Studies

DONALD COWAN, former President, University of Dallas; Fellow, Dallas Institute of Humanities and Cultures

ALONZO A. CRIM, Superintendent, Atlanta Public Schools, Atlanta, Georgia

CLIFTON FADIMAN, Author and critic

DENNIS GRAY, Deputy Director, Council for Basic Education, Washington, D.C.

RICHARD HUNT, Senior Lecturer and Director of the Andrew W. Mellon Faculty Fellowships Program, Harvard University

*Members of the Paideia Group*

# Contents

*Contents*

PART FOUR: BEYOND BASIC SCHOOLING

x

# To Our Readers

THE PAIDEIA PROPOSAL *is addressed to those Americans most concerned with the future of our public schools:*

*To Parents who believe that the decline in the quality of public schooling is damaging the futures of their children.*

*To Teachers troubled that the increasing time spent in keeping basic order in the classroom undermines the real business of schooling: to teach and to learn.*

*To School Boards frightened by the flight of middle-class children and youth to private and parochial schools.*

*To College Educators burdened by the increasing need to provide remedial education which detracts from their ability to offer a meaningful higher education.*

*To Elected Public Officials searching for ways to improve the quality of education without increasing the cost to taxpayers.*

*To Our Readers*

*To Employers concerned about the effects on productivity of a work force lacking skills in reading, writing, speaking, listening, observing, measuring, and computing.*

*To Minority Groups angered by widening gulfs between the better educated and the poorly educated, and between the employed and the unemployed.*

*To Labor Leaders attempting to deal with workers who lack the skills to find jobs in the new high-technology industries.*

*To Military Leaders needing brainpower among the troops capable of coping with sophisticated weaponry.*

*To American Citizens alarmed by the prospects of a democracy in which a declining proportion of the people vote or endeavor to understand the great issues of our time.*

*Such deep and legitimate concerns are addressed by our proposal for the reform of public schooling in America. The reform we seek is designed to improve the opportunities of our youth, the prospects of our economy, and the viability of our democratic institutions. It must be achieved at the community level without resorting to a monolithic, national educational system. It must be, in Lincoln's words, of the people, by the people, and for the people.*

# PART ONE
# The Schooling of a People

# 1
# Democracy and Education

W<small>E ARE</small> on the verge of a new era in our national life. The long-needed educational reform for which this country is at last ready will be a turning point toward that new era.

Democracy has come into its own for the first time in this century. Not until this century have we undertaken to give twelve years of schooling to all our children. Not until this century have we conferred the high office of enfranchised citizenship on all our people, regardless of sex, race, or ethnic origin.

The two—universal suffrage and universal schooling—are inextricably bound together. The one without the other is a perilous delusion. Suffrage without schooling produces mobocracy, not democracy—not rule of law, not constitutional government by the people as well as for them.

The great American educator, John Dewey, recognized this early in this century. In *Democracy and Education*, written in 1916, he first tied these two words together and let each shine light upon the other.

A revolutionary message of that book was that a democratic society must provide equal educational opportunity not only by giving to all its children the same quantity of public education—the same number of years in school—but also by making sure to give to all of them, all with no exceptions, the same quality of education.

The ideal Dewey set before us is a challenge we have failed to meet. It is a challenge so difficult that it is understandable, perhaps excusable, that we have so far failed. But we cannot continue to fail without disastrous consequences for all of us. For the proper working of our political institutions, for the efficiency of our industries and businesses, for the salvation of our economy, for the vitality of our culture, and for the ultimate good of our citizens as individuals, and especially our future citizens—our children—we must succeed.

We are all sufferers from our continued failure to fulfill the educational obligations of a democracy. We are all the victims of a school system that has only gone halfway along the road to realize the promise of democracy.

At the beginning of this century, fewer than 10 percent of those of an age eligible for high school entered such schools. Today, almost 100 percent of our children enter, but not all complete such secondary schooling; many drop out for many reasons, some of them understandable.

It has taken us the better part of eighty years to go halfway toward the goal our society must achieve if it is to be a true democracy. The halfway mark was reached when we finally managed to provide twelve years of basic public schooling for all our children. At that point, we were closer to the goal that Horace Mann set for us more than a century ago when he said: "Education is the gateway to equality."

But the democratic promise of equal educational opportunity, half fulfilled, is worse than a promise broken. It is an ideal betrayed. Equality of educational opportunity is not, in fact, provided if it means no more than taking all the children into the public schools for the same number of hours, days, and years. If once there they are divided into the sheep and the goats, into those destined solely for toil and those destined for economic and political leadership and for a quality of life to which all should have access, then the democratic purpose has been undermined by an inadequate system of public schooling.

It fails because it has achieved only the same quantity of public schooling, not the same quality. This failure is a downright violation of our democratic principles.

We are politically a classless society. Our citizenry as a whole is our ruling class. We should, therefore, be an educationally classless society.

We should have a one-track system of schooling, not a system with two or more tracks, only one of which goes straight ahead while the others shunt the young off onto sidetracks not headed toward the goals our society opens to all. The innermost meaning of social equality is: *sub-*

5

*stantially the same quality of life for all.* That calls for: *the same quality of schooling for all.*

We may take some satisfaction, perhaps, in the fact that we have won half the battle—the quantitative half. But we deserve the full development of the country's human potential. We should, therefore, be vexed that we have not yet gone further. We should be impatient to get on with it, in and through the schools.

Progress toward the fulfillment of democracy by means of our educational system should and can be accelerated. It need not and must not take another century to achieve uniform quality for all in our public schools.

There are signs on all sides that tell us the people want that move forward now. The time is ripe. Parents, teachers, leaders of government, labor unions, corporations—above all, the young themselves—have uttered passionate complaints about the declining quality of public schooling.

There is no acceptable reason why trying to promote equality should have led to a lessening or loss of quality. Two decades after John Dewey, another great American educator, Robert Maynard Hutchins, as much committed to democracy as Dewey was before him, stated the fundamental principle we must now follow in our effort to achieve a true equality of educational conditions. "The best education for the best," he said, "is the best education for all."

6

The shape of the best education for the best is not unknown to us. But we have been slow to learn how to provide it. Nor have we always been honest in our commitment to democracy and its promise of equality. A part of our population—and much too large a part—has harbored the opinion that many of the nation's children are not fully educable. Trainable for one or another job, perhaps, but not educable for the duties of self-governing citizenship and for the enjoyment of things of the mind and spirit that are essential to a good human life.

We must end that hypocrisy in our national life. We cannot say out of one side of our mouth that we are for democracy and all its free institutions including, preeminently, political and civil liberty for all; and out of the other side of our mouth, say that only some of the children—fewer than half—are educable for full citizenship and a full human life.

With the exception of a few suffering from irremediable brain damage, every child is educable up to his or her capacity. Educable—not just trainable for jobs! As John Dewey said almost a century ago, vocational training, training for particular jobs, is not the education of free men and women.

True, children are educable in varying degrees, but the variation in degree must be of the same kind and quality of education. If "the best education for the best is the best education for all," the failure to carry out that principle is the failure on the part of society—a failure of parents, of teachers, of administrators—not a failure on the part of the children.

There are no unteachable children. There are only schools and teachers and parents who fail to teach them.

# 2
# Schooling—Only a Part of Education

I F ALL CHILDREN are educable, all are justified in aspiring to become educated persons. But no one can become fully educated in school, no matter how long the schooling or how good it is. Our concern with education must go beyond schooling.

The schooling of a people does not complete their education. Not even if the quality of schooling were improved to the utmost for all; not even if all who completed twelve years of compulsory basic schooling went on to optional advanced schooling in our colleges and universities and profited by it.

The simple fact is that educational institutions, even at their best, cannot turn out fully educated men and women. The age at which most human beings attend school prevents that. Youth itself is the most serious impediment—in fact, youth is an insuperable obstacle to being an educated person.

No one can be an educated person while immature. It would be a travesty to regard the degrees awarded by our colleges and universities as certifying the completion of education. It is all the more true of the high school diploma.

Only through the trials of adult life, only with the range and depth of experience that makes for maturity, can human beings become educated persons. The mature may not be as trainable as the immature, but they are more educable by virtue of their maturity.

Education is a lifelong process of which schooling is only a small but necessary part. The various stages of schooling reach terminal points. Each can be completed in a definite term of years. But learning never reaches a terminal point. As long as one remains alive and healthy, learning can go on—and should. The body does not continue to grow after the first eighteen or twenty years of life. In fact, it starts to decline after that. But mental, moral, and spiritual growth can go on and should go on for a lifetime.

The ultimate goal of the educational process is to help human beings become educated persons. Schooling is the preparatory stage; it forms the habit of learning and provides the means for continuing to learn after all schooling is completed.

For some, this preparation ends with the completion of basic schooling, amounting to about twelve years. For others, it means the completion of advanced schooling, which may take another four years or more. For all, schooling completed means that education has been begun, but not finished. Schooling, basic or advanced, that does not prepare the individual for further learning has failed, no matter what else it succeeds in doing.

Basic schooling—the schooling compulsory for all—must do something other than prepare some young people for more schooling at advanced levels. It must prepare *all* of them for the continuation of learning in adult life, during their working years and beyond.

How? By imparting to them the skills of learning and giving them the stimulation that will motivate them to keep their minds actively engaged in learning. Schooling should open the doors to the world of learning and provide the guidelines for exploring it.

Basic schooling in America does not now achieve this fundamental objective. It used to do so for those who completed high school at the beginning of this century. With the vastly increased numbers who enter high school now, our system may achieve this objective for a few, but it fails to do it for all. Yet doing it for all is precisely what we mean when we say we want the same quality of schooling for all.

The failure to serve all in this essential respect is one strike against basic schooling in its present deplorable condition. The reform we advocate seeks to remedy that condition. When that is done, the certificate which marks the completion of basic schooling at the end of twelve years will deserve once again to be called what it was called centuries ago—a baccalaureate diploma.

11

In 1817, long before democracy came to full bloom in this country, Thomas Jefferson made a proposal that was radical for his day. He advocated three years of common schooling at the public expense for all the children of Virginia. But he then divided the children into those destined for labor and those destined for learning. Only the latter were to go on further to the local colleges of the time. The rest were to toil on the farms as hired hands or in the shops as apprentices.

In the twentieth century, we demand twelve years of common schooling at public expense for every child in the country. It is no longer a radical demand. But our present tracking system of public schooling still divides children into those destined only for labor and those destined for more schooling.

We believe, on the contrary, that all children are destined for learning, as most are destined for labor by their need to earn a livelihood. To live well in the fullest human sense involves learning as well as earning.

# PART TWO
# The Essentials of Basic Schooling

# 3
## The Same Objectives for All

AT THE VERY HEART of a multitrack system of public schooling lies an abominable discrimination. The system aims at different goals for different groups of children. One goal, higher than the others, is harder to accomplish. The other goals are lower—and perhaps easier, but, ironically, they are all too frequently not attained.

The one-track system of public schooling that *The Paideia Proposal* advocates has the same objectives for all without exception.

These objectives are not now aimed at in any degree by the lower tracks onto which a large number of our underprivileged children are shunted—an educational dead end. It is a dead end because these tracks do not lead to the result that the public schools of a democratic society should seek, first and foremost, for all its children—preparation to go on learning, either at advanced levels of schooling, or in adult life, or both.

Nor, in the present state of our schools, is that main objective aimed at or attained in any satisfactory measure

15

by the higher track along which a minority of favored children move during their years of basic schooling. That track is higher only in the sense that its aims are more difficult to accomplish. But even it is not now directed to the right objectives.

In the early years, before basic schooling branches out in different directions, it fails badly to teach proficiency in the indispensable skills of learning. Even in these years, when it is still a one-track system, it falls far short of delivering the goods.

To achieve the desired quality of democratic education, a one-track system of public schooling for twelve years must aim directly at three main objectives and make every effort to achieve them to a satisfactory degree.

These three objectives are determined by the vocations or callings common to all children when they grow up as citizens, earning their living and putting their free time to good use.

The first of these objectives has already been mentioned. It relates to that aspect of adult life which we call personal growth or self-improvement—mental, moral, and spiritual. Every child should be able to look forward not only to growing up but also to continued growth in all human dimensions throughout life. All should aspire to make as much of their powers as they can. Basic schooling should prepare them to take advantage of every opportunity for personal development that our society offers.

16

A second main objective has to do with another side of adult life—the individual's role as an enfranchised citizen of this republic. Citizens are the principal and permanent rulers of our society. Those elected to public office for a term of years are instrumental and transient rulers—in the service of the citizenry and responsible to the electorate.

The reason why universal suffrage in a true democracy calls for universal public schooling is that the former without the latter produces an ignorant electorate and amounts to a travesty of democratic institutions and processes. To avoid this danger, public schooling must be universal in more than its quantitative aspect. It must be universal also in its qualitative aspect. Hence, the second objective of basic schooling—an adequate preparation for discharging the duties and responsibilities of citizenship.

This requires not only the cultivation of the appropriate civic virtues, but also a sufficient understanding of the framework of our government and of its fundamental principles.

The third main objective takes account of the adult's need to earn a living in one or another occupation.

The twelve years of basic schooling must prepare them for this task, *not* by training them for one or another particular job in our industrial economy, but by giving them the basic skills that are common to all work in a society such as ours.

17

Here then are the three common callings to which all our children are destined: to earn a living in an intelligent and responsible fashion, to function as intelligent and responsible citizens, and to make both of these things serve the purpose of leading intelligent and responsible lives— to enjoy as fully as possible all the goods that make a human life as good as it can be.

To achieve these three goals, basic schooling must have for all a quality that can be best defined, *positively*, by saying that it must be general and liberal; and *negatively*, by saying that it must be nonspecialized and nonvocational.

Describing it as nonvocational may appear to be inconsistent with what has been said about its relation to earning a living. However, the schooling proposed is truly vocational in the sense that it aims to prepare children for the three vocations or callings common to all.

It is truly vocational in a further sense. It will prepare the young for earning a living by enabling them to understand the demands and workings of a technologically advanced society, and to become acquainted with its main occupations. It is nonvocational only in the sense that it does not narrowly train them for one or another particular job.

That kind of specialized or particularized job training at the level of basic schooling is in fact the reverse of something practical and effective in a society that is always changing and progressing. Anyone so trained will have to be retrained when he or she comes to his or her

18

job. The techniques and technology will have moved on since the training in school took place.

Why, then, was such false vocationalism ever introduced into our schools? As the school population rapidly increased in the early decades of this century, educators and teachers turned to something that seemed more appropriate to do with that portion of the school population which they incorrectly and unjustly appraised as being uneducable—only trainable. In doing this, they violated the fundamental democratic maxim of equal educational opportunity.

As compared with narrow, specialized training for particular jobs, general schooling is of the greatest practical value. It is good not only because it is calculated to achieve two of the three main objectives at which basic schooling should aim—preparation for citizenship and for personal development and continued growth. It is also good practically because it will provide preparation for earning a living.

Of all the creatures on earth, human beings are the least specialized in anatomical equipment and in instinctive modes of behavior. They are, in consequence, more flexible than other creatures in their ability to adjust to the widest variety of environments and to rapidly changing external circumstances. They are adjustable to every clime and condition on earth and perpetually adjustable to the shock of change.

That is why general, nonspecialized schooling has the quality that most befits human nature. That is why, in

19

terms of practicality and utility, it is better than any other kind of schooling.

But when we recognize that twelve years of general, nonspecialized schooling for all is the best policy—the most practical preparation for work—we should also realize that that is not its sole justification. It is not only the most expedient kind of schooling, but it is also best for the other reasons stated above: because it prepares our children to be good citizens and to lead good human lives.

# 4
# The Same Course of Study for All

To GIVE THE SAME QUALITY OF SCHOOLING to all requires a program of study that is both liberal and general, and that is, in several, crucial, overarching respects, one and the same for every child. All sidetracks, specialized courses, or elective choices must be eliminated. Allowing them will always lead a certain number of students to voluntarily downgrade their own education.

Elective choices are appropriate only in a curriculum that is intended for different avenues of specialization or different forms of preparation for the professions or technical careers. Electives and specialization are entirely proper at the level of advanced schooling—in our colleges, universities, and technical schools. They are wholly inappropriate at the level of basic schooling.

The course of study to be followed in the twelve years of basic schooling should, therefore, be completely required, with only one exception. That exception is the choice of a second language. In addition to competence in the use of English as everyone's primary language, basic schooling should confer a certain degree of facility in the use of a second language. That second language should be open to elective choice.

The diagram on the opposite page depicts in three columns three distinct modes of teaching and learning, rising in successive gradations of complexity and difficulty from the first to the twelfth year. All three modes are essential to the overall course of study.

These three columns are interconnected, as the diagram indicates. The different modes of learning on the part of the students and the different modes of teaching on the part of the teaching staff correspond to three different ways in which the mind can be improved—(1) by the acquisition of organized knowledge; (2) by the development of intellectual skills; and (3) by the enlargement of understanding, insight, and aesthetic appreciation.

In addition to the three main Columns of Learning, the required course of study also includes a group of auxiliary subjects, of which one is physical education and care of the body. This runs through all twelve years. Of the other two auxiliary subjects, instruction in a variety of manual arts occupies a number of years, but not all twelve; and the third consists of an introduction to the world of work and its range of occupations and careers. It is given in the last two of the twelve years.

COLUMN ONE: ACQUISITION OF KNOWLEDGE

Here are three areas of subject matter indispensable to basic schooling—language, literature, and fine arts;

## The Same Course of Study for All

| | COLUMN ONE | COLUMN TWO | COLUMN THREE |
|---|---|---|---|
| Goals | ACQUISITION OF ORGANIZED KNOWLEDGE | DEVELOPMENT OF INTELLECTUAL SKILLS – SKILLS OF LEARNING | ENLARGED UNDERSTANDING OF IDEAS AND VALUES |
| | by means of | by means of | by means of |
| Means | DIDACTIC INSTRUCTION LECTURES AND RESPONSES TEXTBOOKS AND OTHER AIDS | COACHING, EXERCISES, AND SUPERVISED PRACTICE | MAIEUTIC OR SOCRATIC QUESTIONING AND ACTIVE PARTICIPATION |
| | in three areas of subject-matter | in the operations of | in the |
| Areas Operations and Activities | LANGUAGE, LITERATURE, AND THE FINE ARTS MATHEMATICS AND NATURAL SCIENCE HISTORY, GEOGRAPHY, AND SOCIAL STUDIES | READING, WRITING, SPEAKING, LISTENING CALCULATING, PROBLEM-SOLVING OBSERVING, MEASURING, ESTIMATING EXERCISING CRITICAL JUDGMENT | DISCUSSION OF BOOKS (NOT TEXTBOOKS) AND OTHER WORKS OF ART AND INVOLVEMENT IN ARTISTIC ACTIVITIES e.g., MUSIC, DRAMA, VISUAL ARTS |

THE THREE COLUMNS DO NOT CORRESPOND TO SEPARATE COURSES, NOR IS ONE KIND OF TEACHING AND LEARNING NECESSARILY CONFINED TO ANY ONE CLASS mathematics and natural sciences; history, geography, and social studies.

Why these three? They comprise the most fundamental branches of learning. No one can claim to be educated who is not reasonably well acquainted with all three. They provide the learner with indispensable knowledge about nature and culture, the world in which we live, our social institutions,and ourselves.

The traditional name for the mode of instruction here is "didactic," or "teaching by telling." It employs textbooks and other instructional materials and is accompanied by laboratory demonstrations. The mind here is improved by the acquisition of organized knowledge.

Instruction in language comprises the learning of grammar and syntax, the forms of discourse, and to some extent the history of our own language. Comparisons between English and other languages being studied in the program should be stressed. Whether mathematics is also a language and how it compares with a natural language such as English should be considered.

Instruction in mathematics, beginning with simple arithmetic in the first grade, should rise to at least one year of calculus. It should be integrated from the very beginning with instruction in the use of calculators and lead subsequently to at least introductory instruction in the use of, and programming for, computers.

Instruction in the natural sciences includes physics, chemistry, and biology. Their interconnectedness and interdependence are stressed. Such instruction does not begin formally in the early grades but preparation for it can be made in a variety of attractive ways from the beginning.

History and geography are to be understood as including our knowledge of human and social affairs, not only within the boundaries of our own nation, but with regard to the rest of the world. Preparation for the formal study of history should begin in the early grades by storytelling and biographical narratives but, when formal study begins, it should be sequential and systematic, combining a narration of events with knowledge of social, political, and economic institutions and diverse phases of cultural development.

The innovative aspect of the first column lies not in the choice of subject matter but in the concentration and continuity of the study required. Those who know how inadequate and fragmentary is the knowledge offered to a large majority of those now graduating from high school will recognize the importance of our emphasis on these requirements.

## COLUMN TWO: DEVELOPMENT OF SKILL

Here are the basic skills of learning—competence in the *use* of language, primarily English, aided by facility in a second language, as well as competence in dealing with a wide range of symbolic devices, such as calculators, computers, and scientific instruments.

25

The skills to be acquired are the skills of *reading, writing, speaking, listening, observing, measuring, estimating,* and *calculating.* They are linguistic, mathematical, and scientific skills. They are the skills that everyone needs in order to learn anything, in school or elsewhere. Without them, it is impossible to go on learning by one's self, whether for pleasure, or to qualify for a new job, or to be promoted in the present one.

It will be noted that language and mathematics appear in both Columns One and Two, but their significance is different in each. In Column One, *knowledge about* mathematics and language is acquired; in Column Two, the student learns *how to do* mathematical operations correctly and how to use language effectively for communication. "Know-how" consists in skilled performance. It differs from "knowledge about," which consists in knowing that something is the thus-and-so, and not otherwise.

The development of the Column Two skills clearly has close connections with the study of the three fundamental areas of subject matter in Column One. Only to the degree that pupils develop these skills, and form the habit of using them, can instruction in language and literature, mathematics and natural science, history and geography be successful.

Skills cannot be acquired in a vacuum. They must be practiced in the very study of the three basic areas of subject matter, as well as in the process of acquiring linguistic competence, competence in communication, com-

26

petence in the handling of symbolic devices, and competence in critical thinking.

Since what is learned here is skill in performance, not knowledge of facts and formulas, the mode of teaching cannot be didactic. It cannot consist in the teacher telling, demonstrating, or lecturing. Instead, it must be akin to the coaching that is done to impart athletic skills. A coach does not teach simply by telling or giving the learner a rule book to follow. A coach trains by helping the learner to *do,* to go through the right motions, and to organize a sequence of acts in a correct fashion. He corrects faulty performance again and again and insists on repetition of the performance until it achieves a measure of perfection.

Only in this way can skill in reading, writing, speaking, and listening be acquired. Only in this way can a similar measure of skill be acquired in mathematical and scientific operations. Only in this way can the ability to think critically—to judge and to discriminate—be developed. When coaching is not adequately undertaken, little can be expected in the development of the basic skills.

Coaching involves a different teacher-pupil relationship and a different pupil-teacher ratio than does instruction by telling and by the use of textbooks.

The innovative aspect of Column Two in the basic course of study lies in the fact that nowadays effective coaching and drilling is much too frequently absent from basic schooling. The lack of coaching and drilling by itself accounts for the present deficiencies of many high school graduates in reading, writing, computing, and in following directions.

It is evident that Column Two is the backbone of basic schooling. Proficiency in all the skills that it lists—all of them the very means of learning itself—is indispensable to the efficient teaching and learning of the subject matters in Column One; and also indispensable to teaching and learning in Column Three.

Acquiring facility in the use of a second language is included in Column Two. Among modern languages, a choice can be made of French, German, Italian, Spanish, Russian, Chinese, and possibly others; it may even extend to Latin and Greek. A second language serves to enlarge the scope of the student's understanding of the culture in which English is the primary language by introducing him or her to the imagery and conceptual framework of the cultures that employ these other languages.

## COLUMN THREE: ENLARGEMENT OF THE UNDERSTANDING

Here we have a mode of teaching and learning that has all too rarely been attempted in the public schools. Columns One and Two have important innovative aspects when compared with what now goes on and is either largely or totally left out. Column Three is virtually all innovative.

The materials of learning in Column Three can be described by calling them, on the one hand, books—books that are *not* textbooks—and, on the other hand, products of human artistry. The books are of every kind—historical, scientific, philosophical, poems, stories, essays. The products of human artistry include individual pieces of music, of visual art, plays, and productions in dance, film, or television. The emphasis throughout is on the individual work.

The mode of learning in Column Three engages the mind in the study of individual works of merit, whether literary or otherwise, accompanied by a discussion of the ideas, the values, and the forms embodied in such products of human art.

The appropriate mode of instruction in Column Three is neither didactic nor coaching. It cannot be teaching by telling and by using textbooks. It cannot consist in supervising the activities involved in acquiring skills.

It must be the Socratic mode of teaching, a mode of teaching called "maieutic" because it helps the student bring ideas to birth. It is teaching by asking questions, by leading discussions, by helping students to raise their minds up from a state of understanding or appreciating less to a state of understanding or appreciating more.

The interrogative or discussion method of teaching to be employed in Column Three stimulates the imagination and intellect by awakening the creative and inquisitive powers. In no other way can children's understanding of what they know be improved, and their appreciation of cultural objects be enhanced.

The books in Column Three—fiction, poetry, essays, history, science, and philosophy—serve a twofold purpose.

On the one hand, discussion draws on the student's skills of reading, writing, speaking, and listening, and uses them to sharpen the ability to think clearly, critically, and reflectively. It teaches participants how to analyze their own minds as well as the thought of others, which is to say it engages students in disciplined conversation about ideas and values.

On the other hand, discussion introduces students to the fundamental ideas in the basic subject matters of Column One, and especially the ideas underlying our form of government and the institutions of our society.

To fulfill the objective of preparing all young people to become intelligent citizens requires the careful reading and discussion of at least the following documents: the Declaration of Independence, the Constitution, selections from the *Federalist Papers*, and the Gettysburg Address. Other books will fill this purpose out, but these few are basic to understanding our democracy.

For mutual understanding and responsible debate among the citizens of a democratic community, and for differences of opinion to be aired and resolved, citizens must be able to communicate with one another in a common language. "Language" in this sense involves a common vocabulary of ideas. This common intellectual resource is theirs only if they have read, discussed, and come to understand a certain number of books that deal with the ideas operative in the life of their time and place.

Music and other works of art can be dealt with in seminars in which ideas are discussed; but, like poetry and fiction, they need an additional treatment in order to be appreciated aesthetically—to be enjoyed and admired for their excellence. In this connection, exercises in the performance and composition of poetry, music, and visual works, as well as in the production of dramatic works, will help develop that appreciation in the most direct manner.

The best way to understand a play is to act in it, or at least to read it out loud. The best way to understand a piece of music is to sing or play it. The best way to understand a work of dance is to try to dance it. Participation in the creation of works of art is as important as viewing, listening to, and discussing them. All children should have such pleasurable experiences.

THE INTEGRATION OF THE THREE COLUMNS

We have noted earlier the interplay between Columns One and Two. It can now be seen how Column Three supplements and reinforces the learning that is accomplished in the other two columns.

The reading of books throughout the twelve years of basic schooling, from easy books and mainly imaginative works in the early grades to more difficult books and expository as well as imaginative in the upper grades acquaints the growing mind with fundamental ideas in the subject matters of Column One, and at the same time employs and perfects all the linguistic skills of Column Two.

Without coaching, learners will lack the skills needed for the study of the basic subject matters. Without discussion, they may be memorizing machines, able to pass

31

quizzes or examinations. But probe their minds and you will find that what they know by memory, they do not understand.

They have spent hours in classrooms where they were talked at, where they recited and took notes, plus hours (often too few) of homework poring over textbooks, extracting facts to commit to memory. But when have their minds been addressed, in what connection have they been called upon to think for themselves, to respond to important questions and to raise them themselves, to pursue an argument, to defend a point of view, to understand its opposite, to weigh alternatives?

There is little joy in most of the learning they are now compelled to do. Too much of it is make-believe, in which neither teacher nor pupil can take a lively interest. Without some joy in learning—a joy that arises from hard work well done and from the participation of one's mind in a common task—basic schooling cannot initiate the young into the life of learning, let alone give them the skill and the incentive to engage in it further. Only the student whose mind has been engaged in thinking for itself is an active participant in the learning process that is essential to basic schooling.

Without what is called for in Column Three, such participation cannot be accomplished to any satisfactory degree. It is not now accomplished at all for most of the students in our public schools, and it is accomplished to an insufficient degree for even the chosen few.

32

## THE AUXILIARY STUDIES

Young people need physical exercise for their health's sake and also as an outlet for their abundant energy. Twelve years of physical education and participation in various intramural sports and athletic exercises are provided to fill this need. The program should be accompanied by instruction about health.

For a number of years, fewer than all twelve, boys and girls alike should participate in a wide variety of manual activities, including typing, cooking, sewing, wood- and metalworking, crafts using other materials, automobile driving and repair, maintenance of electrical and other household equipment, and so on.

In the later years, they should receive instruction to prepare them for choosing and finding a career. This is not to be done by requiring them to make a premature choice of a job and by giving them training for that particular job. Rather, the young person should be introduced to the wide range of human work—the kinds of occupations and careers, their significance and requirements, their rewards and opportunities.

If, over and above such general preparation, individuals need training for particular jobs that do not require the kind of advanced schooling that is appropriate to four-year colleges and universities with their technical and professional schools, this can be obtained after basic schooling is completed in two-year community colleges, in technical institutes, or on the job itself.

33

All activities and interests not included in the program as set forth should be regarded as extracurricular, to be engaged in voluntarily in afterschool hours.

---

The program recommended in the preceding pages is offered as a model. It can be adapted in a variety of ways to the diverse circumstances of different schools or school systems. *Our recommendation is not a monolithic program to be adopted uniformly everywhere.*

But the model does insist, for its validity, on the presence in all schools or school systems of the Three Columns—on the establishing of the three modes of learning and the three modes of teaching. The precise way in which that is to be accomplished will be determined by school boards and administrators in the light of the populations with which they are dealing and with reference to a variety of other relevant circumstances.

The system of public education in this country has always been pluralistic and should remain so. Preserving pluralism need not and should not prevent the adoption by *all* our schools of the central features of our model as an ideal to be realized in a variety of specifically different ways.

This cannot be conscientiously accomplished simply by introducing in some form the Three Columns of Learning. It also calls for the elimination of many things that now clutter up the school day. At the very least, their elimination is necessary to make room for what should displace them.

It eliminates all specialized training for particular jobs.

It eliminates from the curriculum and puts into the category of optional extracurricular activities a variety of pastimes that contribute little to education in comparison with the time, energy, and money spent on them.

If it did not call for all these displacements and eliminations, there would not be enough time in the school day or the school year to accomplish everything that is essential to the general, nonspecialized learning that must be the content of basic schooling.

Programs closely akin to what is here proposed have been instituted in other countries. Something like what is here proposed is carried on in our own country in a few exceptional schools, public and private.

Those who think the proposed course of study cannot be successfully followed by all children fail to realize that the children of whom they are thinking have never had their minds challenged by requirements such as these. It is natural for children to rise to meet higher expectations; but only if those expectations are set before them, and made both reasonable and attractive. They will respond when their minds are challenged by teachers able to give the different types of instruction set forth earlier, and who are themselves vitally interested in what they are teaching.

Worse evils than ignorance, lack of discipline, deficiency in rudimentary skills, and impoverished understanding result from most of the existing programs of

35

instruction in our public schools. The absence of intellectual stimulation and the failure to challenge students by
expecting the most of them leads to boredom, delin-
quency, lawless violence, drug dependence, alcoholism,
and other forms of undesirable conduct.

Unless the overflowing energies of young people are
fully and constructively employed, they will spill over into
all forms of antisocial and destructive behavior. Their
energies can be employed constructively only by a program of studies that engages their minds, that demands
their taking an active part in learning, and that pushes
and helps all to reach out and up for as much as they can
get out of school.

*The Paideia Proposal* will be followed by a book of
essays entitled *The Paideia Program: Pointers and Prospects*. This will provide guidelines for putting the program into effect.

# 5
# Overcoming Initial Impediments

A<small>T THIS POINT</small> the reader may be provoked to ask: "Isn't it obvious that the homes and environments from which children come to school will give some a distinct advantage in pursuing the program, while others will suffer from equally distinct disadvantages? Does not defective or even adverse nurturing in the years before schooling (and also afterwards) set up impediments that must be overcome?"

Yes, it is obvious, and we think something can be done about it.

The hopeful fact is that from the moment of birth children are capable of learning. They are born with the desire as well as the need to know. That desire—natural curiosity—can be nourished or it can be starved. The failure to nourish it as early as possible has dire consequences for the child's later schooling and adult life.

The individual's innate disposition to learn can be put to use in infancy and early childhood. It is then that neglect by parents or adverse circumstance maims or crushes this natural capacity. Preschool deprivation is the cause of backwardness or failure in school.

Schooling cannot do the job it should do equally well for all children if some are adequately prepared for school and some are not.

For the school to succeed in giving the same quality of basic education to all children, all must be prepared for it in roughly equal measure. Hence, at least one year—or better, two or three years—of preschool tutelage must be provided for those who do not get such preparation from favorable environments.

The idea behind the Head Start experiment was, indeed, a sound one. Preparation for schooling is not a dispensable accessory to the reform we are proposing. It is an essential ingredient, strongly recommended wherever it appears necessary and expedient.

A democratic society, defined as an ideal to be approximated, is one in which all, being equal in their humanity, enjoy equality of treatment. But in actuality a democratic society is limited in its ability to effect such equality. It can do so only through the public agencies it is able to finance and over which it can exercise some control. Preschool tutelage should, therefore, be provided at public expense for those who need but cannot afford it.

The home is a private, not a public, institution. The inequality of homes produces inequalities of nurture that lead some to draw wrong conclusions about the abilities of children. Instead of seeing them as differing only in the degree to which they have a present or future capacity for learning, they divide them into those who are truly educable and those who are not. This division is then used to

38

justify our not trying to give all the children the same quality of schooling. We keep all in school for the same number of years, but do not accord them equal treatment.

The sooner a democratic society intervenes to remedy the cultural inequality of homes and environments, the sooner it will succeed in fulfilling the democratic mandate of equal educational opportunity for all.

Without preparation for schooling, the chances of success in any attempted reform of the public school are greatly diminished. Without it, the country may even continue to believe the self-defeating doctrine that says not all children are educable and only some deserve the best quality of schooling we can afford.

# 6
# Individual Differences

ANOTHER OBJECTION to the feasibility of our proposed reform is that we have overlooked a central fact. We have apparently dismissed as irrelevant the fact of individual differences. If it is not this oversight of a real obstacle with which we will be charged, then it will be our apparently thoughtless neglect of individual differences as if they did not matter, as if they had no significant bearing on the educability of the young.

"You propose," the objectors may say, "the same educational objectives for all the children." Yes, that is precisely what we propose.

"You propose the same course of study for all, and with no electives throughout the twelve years." Yes, again, that is right.

"You propose that they shall all complete this required course of study with a satisfactory standard of accomplishment regardless of native ability, temperamental bent, or conscious preferences." Yes, yes, yes!

How utopian! How outlandish! It will never work! At best it might suit the fortunate few, an elite who can measure up to what is required and who can acquit themselves with honors. But for the rest, it is pie in the sky, miles beyond their reach. To call it the kind of educational program that democracy demands and deserves is fine talk, but all the fine talk in the world cannot overcome the facts that stare us in the face when we pay a moment's attention to the actual population of our schools.

Why, anyhow, this unrelieved emphasis on *sameness* when the most obvious facts are the *manifold differences* among people—differences of all sorts, in native ability, in interests and inclinations, in temperament, in every taste and aptitude for learning, in home upbringing, in economic status and opportunity, in ethnic and racial heritage, and so on? Whether these differences are innate or acquired, whether they exist at birth or are produced by nurture and environment, is not the point. There they are. Any program of basic schooling that does not take them into account flies in the face of facts that will defeat it.

What the skeptics and scoffers forget are the samenesses in the context of which these differences exist. So we must, first of all, remind the objectors of those other facts—facts more significant than the differences upon which they dwell. Facts are facts, and calling attention to one set of facts does not justify forgetting, overlooking, or dismissing another set.

Despite their manifold individual differences, the children are all the same in their human nature. They are human beings and their human equality consists in the fact that no child is more or less human than another.

Their sameness as human beings—as members of the same species—means that every child has all the distinguishing properties common to all members of the species. They all have the same inherent tendencies, the same inherent powers, the same inherent capacities. The fact that individuals possess these common traits to different degrees is itself proof that they share a common nature at the same time that they differ in degree in the many ways that make each a unique individual. Individual differences are always and only differences in degree, never differences in kind.

In our democratic society, moreover, all children can look forward to a future that is the same in a number of essential respects. All will grow up to become full-fledged citizens with suffrage and with the political liberty it confers. All can demand to have their human and civil rights protected by the Constitution and by the laws that conform to it.

Those rights include preeminently rights to whatever conditions are needed for the pursuit of happiness—needed for their making the most of themselves and for their living as well as possible. They all have a right to participate in the general economic welfare and to expect a decent standard of living with enough free time to make a good life for themselves.

These are the facts of sameness that justify the sameness of the objectives at which our program for basic schooling aims. These are the facts of sameness that justify requiring the same course of study for all and a satisfactory standard of accomplishment for all.

43

To insist upon these facts—facts too often overlooked or ignored—is not to overlook or ignore individual differences.

What, then, must be done to temper the same to the different—to cope with individual differences?

The answer lies not in any retreat from the sameness of the program, any watering down of it, any deceptions that make it look as if it were the same for all while, in fact, it has become a two-track or a multitrack system.

The answer lies in adjusting that program to individual differences by administering it sensitively and flexibly in ways that accord with whatever differences must be taken into account. Children who, in one way or another, manifest deficiencies that would result in their not achieving the requisite standard of performance must be given special help to overcome those deficiencies. Such help would be truly remedial—remedying individual deficiencies that can and must be overcome.

What in recent years has been called remedial teaching is for the most part an effort to remedy defects that result from educational failures at prior levels of instruction. Because children were not taught what they should have been taught, or not taught well enough, the resultant defects must be remedied. What we here are calling for is remedial in another sense. It presupposes that in the course of study the subjects to be taught will be taught and taught well. But it recognizes that some children need more time or more help because of deficiencies that can be overcome by special efforts on the part of teachers and

44

parents—and the children themselves—to deal with their individual difficulties.

It may be that a considerable number of children will require such remedial teaching for a number of years. It may be that such remedial teaching will be most needed in the earlier rather than the later years of the program; but it should be available whenever it is needed so that no child is ever allowed to fall irremediably behind as is now the case.

We once again express our faith that there is no un-educable child—no unteachable child. There are only children that we fail to teach in a way that befits their individual condition. That faith rejects with abhorrence the notion that there are any irremediable deficiencies to block the attainment of the same educational goals for all.

Our program is not utopian. It is more realistic than the schooling that magnifies and overreacts to individual differences, that accepts deficiencies as irremediable, and that makes a mockery of equal educational opportunity by failing to recognize and make the best use of the same-nesses that underlie the differences.

# PART THREE
# Teaching and Learning

# 7
# The Heart of the Matter

THE PROCLAMATION OF PRINCIPLES, the setting of common objectives, the requirement of a well-devised course of study, the maintenance of reasonable standards of achievement—clearly, these are the essentials of the desired basic schooling for all.

But they are external prerequisites to be fulfilled. Fulfilling them, however necessary, is not enough. They are the outer structure, not the heart of the matter.

The heart of the matter is the quality of the learning that goes on during the hours spent in class and during the time spent doing assigned homework.

The course of study is nothing but a series of channels or conduits. The child goes in at one end and comes out at the other. The difference between what goes in and what comes out depends upon the quality of learning and of teaching that takes place throughout the journey.

The quality of learning, in turn, depends very largely on the quality of the teaching—teaching that guides and inspires learning in the classroom, and that directs and motivates learning to be done in homework. Largely but not entirely! Effective learning often occurs in spite of defective teaching. Teaching at its best is only an aid to learning, but that aid is most needed by those who are least adept at learning.

All genuine learning is active, not passive. It involves the use of the mind, not just the memory. It is a process of discovery, in which the student is the main agent, not the teacher.

How does a teacher aid discovery and elicit the activity of the student's mind? By inviting and entertaining questions, by encouraging and sustaining inquiry, by supervising helpfully a wide variety of exercises and drills, by leading discussions, by giving examinations that arouse constructive responses, not just the making of check marks on printed forms.

Learning by discovery can occur without help, but only geniuses can educate themselves without the help of teachers. For most students, learning by discovery must be aided. That is where teachers come in—as aids in the process of learning by discovery, not as knowers who attempt to put the knowledge they have in their minds into the minds of their pupils.

That never can be done, certainly not with good or permanent results. Teachers may think they are stuffing minds, but all they are ever affecting is the memory. Nothing can ever be forced into anyone's mind except by brainwashing, which is the very opposite of genuine teaching.

Teachers who do not understand these truths mis-understand the true character of learning. Worse, they do violence to the minds in their care. By assuming that they are the primary cause of learning on the part of their pupils, by filling passive receptacles, they act merely as indoctrinators—overseers of memorization—but they are not teachers

How should teachers—functioning properly as aids to learning—work to guide or assist the activity of the pupil's mind, the activity that is the principal cause of learning?

The answer differs according to the three ways in which learning improves the mind: (1) by the acquisition of information or organized knowledge; (2) by the development of intellectual skills; (3) by the enlargement of the understanding.

In each of these three modes of learning, there is a different kind of help to be given by the teacher.

Insofar as information and organized knowledge can be acquired from textbooks or manuals, teachers help such learning by monitoring its acquisition by drills, exercises, and tests. Their help also takes the form of didactic instruction, that is, lecturing: by telling, explaining, or pointing out the difficulties to be overcome, the problems to be solved, the connections and conclusions to be learned.

To keep this sort of teaching from becoming no more than a temporary stuffing of the memory, the telling should be tempered by questioning—back and forth across the teacher's desk. The more there is questioning and discussion, the more enlivened the class hour and the better the understanding of the subject being taught.

The development of the intellectual skills—the skills of learning itself—requires a different kind of help from teachers. Here (as we have said) the teacher must function the way athletic coaches do. John Dewey's oft-repeated but oft-misunderstood maxim that learning is by doing applies here most crucially and should govern the teaching effort.

What John Dewey had in mind was not exclusively physical doing or even social doing—engagement in practical projects of one kind or another. The most important kind of doing, so far as learning is concerned, is intellectual or mental doing. In other words, one can learn to read or write well only by reading and writing, one can learn to measure and calculate well only by measuring and calculating, just as one learns to swim or run well only by swimming or running.

To learn how to do any of these things well, one must not only engage in doing them, but one must be guided in doing them by someone more expert in doing them than oneself.

That more expert person is a teacher, who coaches and drills. Coaching requires, for at least part of the time, individual attention, but it can also be done with groups of learners if the groups are small enough to allow the coach to give individual attention where it is needed.

The third kind of learning which aims at raising the mind up from a lesser or weaker understanding to a stronger and fuller one cannot rely on telling or coaching. Here the teacher teaches by asking, not telling, and by using materials other than textbooks or manuals.

Discussion, in which the students both ask and answer questions, must prevail. In discussion the teacher must be keenly aware of the ways in which insights occur to enlarge the understanding—ways that differ from individual to individual. That demands close attention to what is happening in the student's mind as he or she asks or answers questions, and as one question or answer leads to another.

These three kinds of learning and teaching cannot take place effectively in the same kinds of classrooms or under exactly the same external conditions. To impose a uniform classroom setting, uniform class size, or uniform class hours on all three modes of instruction is to neglect and nullify their differences.

The ordinary classroom, with students sitting in rows and the teacher standing in front of them, dominating it, and the ordinary class period running for fifty minutes, properly serve the purposes of didactic instruction, but nothing else. Applied to the other two types of instruction, it will defeat them completely.

Consider the gymnasium, where athletic coaching is done. How does it permit the quite different relationship between the coach and those whose skill is to be trained?

By enabling the teacher to move from one trainee to another, standing or sitting beside the learner, spending more time with this one than with that one, and demanding of some or all more time for repeated exercises than an ordinary class period allows.

In other than physical education, exercising and practicing during after-school hours may well be required to meet the needs of the coaching teacher. When such homework is done, it must be carefully examined and corrected by the teacher. Without that, it comes to nothing. Moreover, parental support of homework is needed to see that it is done effectively. We are the only country in the world that is lax in this respect. No other country asks so little work of its children as we do. Some of our school "days" are over by noon and homework—not much of it at that—has become the exception.

Teaching by discussion imposes still other requirements. For older children, it calls for more than a fifty-minute class period. It also calls for a room in which the participants in the discussion sit around a table instead of in rows. The teacher is one of the participants, not the principal performer standing up in front of the group.

The teacher's role in discussion is to keep it going along fruitful lines—by moderating, guiding, correcting, leading, and arguing like one more *student!* The teacher is first among equals. All must have the sense that they are participating as equals, as is the case in a genuine conversation.

54

In all three ways of learning, the more active the learner the better. As far as possible, passivity must be discouraged and overcome. This does not mean more activity on the part of the teacher, but a different kind of activity from that which most teachers now display when they go on the assumption that teaching is transferring the contents of their own minds (or their notes) into the minds of their pupils.

Finally, a word must be said about deportment. Laxity in this respect can be completely destructive of learning and completely frustrating to the efforts of the best teachers. Students must be required to behave in class and in school in a manner that is conducive to learning.

Infraction of rules of conduct devised for this purpose must be effectively dealt with. Where discipline breaks down, where offenses against teachers or fellow students go unpunished, schools and classrooms are places where little or no effective learning and no teaching can take place.

Disturbing the peace is a serious matter in school as it is on the street—perhaps even more serious. Unquestionably, the well-taught class that awakens lively interest in learning and gives students a sense of accomplishment will help to promote decorum. But at all times it is of the first importance to let children know what is expected of them. The clearer and higher the expectations, the better the response.

Much has been said in recent years about the importance of the school in developing the moral character as well as the mind. One thing is certain. It is not by preaching moral homilies or by giving little lessons in ethics that moral character is formed. The moral sense develops under the discipline and examples that define desirable behavior. This must be supported by stern measures to check or prevent misconduct.

# 8
# The Preparation of Teachers

THERE ARE AND ALWAYS WILL BE a relatively small number of highly gifted, strongly motivated teachers who manage, in spite of all adverse conditions, to perform creditably, even magnificently. But that number is far from enough to achieve the desired quality of teaching for all. At present, many factors work against having enough good teachers to staff our schools.

The surroundings in which many teachers work, especially in our large urban schools, would turn any other work place into a shambles. The productivity would drop below the lowest level for survival in business. It is not surprising that the level of achievement in many of our public schools falls below the comparable minimum.

Bad working conditions are not the only reason why we do not have enough able teachers, or why good ones are prevented from performing as they should. Recruiting for the profession is hampered by the average rate of pay, which is often less than that in other less taxing lines of work. Not only do we pay our teachers too little for work they are expected to do, we also fail in this country to give them the respect that the worth of their service to the community deserves. Teachers in the United States do not enjoy the social status that the importance of their position merits.

Add to all this the many administrative, public relations, and quasi-menial duties that teachers are asked to perform, duties that take mind and energy away from teaching, and it is easy to understand why our educational system is not able to attract many of the ablest young into the teaching profession, or to turn those who do join the ranks into adequate teachers.

Everything that has been said so far cites negative and external factors—bad working conditions, compensation that is too low, inferior social status, distracting demands. But there is more. Were all these negative factors eliminated or rectified, positive factors and conditions for training and holding a sufficiently large number of good teachers must be provided.

Nobody would expect all teachers to be truly educated persons—persons who possessed the requisite knowledge and understanding and were also skilled to a high degree in the art of teaching. That would be a utopian ideal. No amount of schooling, as was said earlier, can produce an educated person. To be truly educated is a state achieved by self-direction, usually long after schooling is completed, in the later years of life.

That being so, what is the goal to be aimed at, one that is practical rather than utopian? It is that teachers should be *on the way* to becoming educated persons. What signs indicate their tending in this direction? One is that they manifest competence as learners. Another is that they show a sufficiently strong interest in their own education and a sufficiently strong motivation to carry on learning while engaged in teaching.

To expect every teacher to learn in the course of every day's teaching is again utopian. But it is not utopian to expect intellectual growth in every term of teaching. The teacher who has stopped learning is a deadening influence rather than a help to students being initiated into the ways of learning.

If these are the touchstones of competence in teaching, what sort of schooling should be prescribed for those wishing to enter the profession of teaching and to practice it at the level of basic schooling?

They should themselves be at least as well-schooled as the graduates of the schools in which they are expecting to teach. They should have completed the required course of study we have recommended. Many teachers now employed in our public schools have not themselves had basic schooling of this quality, or even of the quality now provided in our better schools.

Even if all had the basic schooling that we are advocating, it would not be enough. Our future teachers should go on to take college work of the same kind at a higher level, that is, follow a course of study that is general, liberal, and humanistic. That course of study will add to their knowledge, develop their intellectual powers, and enlarge their understanding beyond the level of attainment set for

59

basic schooling. Nothing less than this will start them on the way to becoming educated persons—our first and indispensable requirement for competent teachers.

The course of study here proposed for the preparation of teachers does not include most or much of what is now taught to college students who plan to teach and specialize for it by taking their majors in departments of education or in teachers colleges.

The present teacher-training programs turn out persons who are not sufficiently equipped with the knowledge, the intellectual skills, or the developed understanding needed to guide and help the young in the course of study we have recommended.

If all children are expected to learn what is prescribed in our curriculum, it is reasonable to expect their teachers to be able to teach not just this or that portion, but all of it. Hence they should have a college education other than that which requires majoring or specializing in the subjects now required for teacher certification.

Do those who plan to teach in the twelve years of basic schooling need any specialized training? Yes, but it should come *after* they have completed a general college education, either in graduate courses in a university department or school of education or in what is comparable to internship in medicine—practice teaching under supervision.

Teaching is one of the three great cooperative arts. The other two are farming and healing—the arts of agriculture and of medicine. All three are "cooperative" be-

60

cause they must work with nature to produce the goods they aim at.

The cooperative art of the farmer consists in making the best use of seed, soil, and weather to produce the livestock, grains, or fruits that nature is able to produce alone, without the farmer's help. The cooperative art of the physician consists in employing the body's own resources for healing—for maintaining or regaining health.

The cooperative art of the teacher depends on the teacher's understanding of how the mind learns by the exercise of its own powers, and on his or her use of this understanding to help the minds of others to learn.

Obviously, the future teacher's own experience in learning is indispensable to such an understanding. It is by the skillful use of this self-understanding that the teacher can help others to learn. This skillfulness is developed best by practice under supervision; that is, by coaching. All the skills of teaching are intellectual skills that can be developed only by coaching, not by lecture courses in pedagogy and teaching methods such as are now taught in most schools or departments of education and are now required for certification.

One final condition must be mentioned. The effectiveness of even the best trained teachers will depend on the role played by the principal of the school in which they teach.

# 9
# The Principal

THE SCHOOL IS A COMMUNITY. Not so, a school district or a school system. These are collections or aggregates of school communities in one locality. For this reason, the role of the school principal differs from that of the other administrators of a school system.

Like any community, the school community needs government. It needs leadership. Its affairs, internal and external, must be administered from day to day, from moment to moment. But the school is not an ordinary community like a city or state. It is a community devoted to learning, and its citizens are teachers and students engaged in that acitivity. It must also be conceived as including the parents whose cooperation with the school is essential to its success.

These things being so, the head of the school—its administrator—should not be solely or even primarily concerned with running the school efficiently or economically, or merely with keeping the peace of the community. Keeping the peace, doing justice, balancing budgets, enforcing laws is the main business of the political community at any level; they are not the *main business* of the school community. Its main business is teaching and learning. The head of the school—its principal—should, therefore, administer all other affairs in ways that facilitate the *main business*.

What does this mean? How does this redefine the role of the school principal?

The person chosen for that position should be a notably competent and dedicated teacher, with much classroom experience. It is not enough for the incumbent to be familiar with the administrative regulations, expert in bureaucratic procedures, and gifted with political acumen, important though such qualifications may be. The principal must be first and foremost what the title implies—the head teacher, or what in private schools is called the headmaster, leader of the other teachers who are also called masters. They are so called because they once were *masters* of the liberal arts.

The principal need not actually engage in teaching, though he or she will find it desirable from time to time. What is all important is that the principal provide the educational leadership that the school community needs. It has been shown in repeated studies that the quality of teaching and learning that goes on in a school is largely determined by the quality of such leadership.

Educational leadership by the principal is at present rare. Things being as they are, the principal has neither the time nor the inclination, even supposing the competence, to provide the leadership so sorely needed. Its character will, of course, vary with different schools in different places. But two conditions would appear to be linked with effective performance in the role of principal.

One is that he or she should have authority to hire and fire teachers (in consultation with faculty representatives and with regard for due process as set forth in administrative rules and union regulations). As a corollary, the principal should also have a voice—preferably a controlling voice—in assignments and promotions, so that these take place in a way most likely to advance the educational objectives of the school.

A second condition is that the principal should have the authority and be given the power to enforce standards of conduct—that measure of decorum and good behavior on the part of the student body that is indispensable to learning and teaching. It is not only necessary for the principal to have such disciplinary powers; it is also necessary for parents to recognize the principal's authority in enforcing rules of conduct that make the school community a safe and sane place for learning.

# PART FOUR
# Beyond Basic Schooling

# 10
## Higher Learning

"THE GOAL at which any phase of education, true to itself, should aim," John Dewey declared, "is more education. Other objectives may surround that goal, but it is central."

For those whose schooling ends after twelve years, that basic phase has prepared them for adult learning beyond all schooling. For others, it has prepared them not solely for adult learning but also for more schooling of an advanced kind, in the so-called institutions of higher education: colleges, universities, and technical schools.

The education that takes place there is often called the higher learning. It would be more appropriate to refer to it as further learning, for there is still more education to be had and further learning to be done, beyond the higher learning.

Under whatever name, these higher institutions have been severely crippled by the inadequate preparation of those who successfully apply for entrance. The improvement of basic schooling, by which we seek to raise its quality for all, will also do much more that is to be desired. It will prepare and motivate more young people to go on to college, and this enlarged and better-prepared student body will enable our colleges to raise their sights and to become the centers of higher education that they profess to be.

As things are now, they are hampered by the need to remedy the deficiencies of basic schooling. Instead of being able to rely on acquired knowledge, skills, and understanding and to build on our Three Columns of Learning, they are now compelled to teach all kinds of elementary work, to do what should have been done years earlier. Subjects supposedly learned in the upper years of basic schooling must be taught, or retaught, in college. Time must be spent in catching up with the deficiencies in reading, writing, speaking, computing, as well as doing something about poor or nonexistent habits of study.

Relieved of these burdens, our colleges would be in a position to reconceive their role. They would have the opportunity to recast the forms of higher education. Among these, two main purposes suggest themselves as appropriate for collegiate schooling to serve.

One is preparation for a vocation that requires specialized knowledge and technical training. With reformed lower schools, this could be accomplished in college, though for those going on to certain professions, further study in graduate, professional, or technical schools will be required.

70

The second purpose is the pursuit of general learning itself by students who are older and can build on their basic schooling to do more advanced work.

Those going to college to prepare themselves for vocations requiring specialized knowledge and technical training should be able to choose among a wide variety of programs. But, in addition to such elective majors, there should be for all a required minor course of study that will carry them to levels of general, liberal, and humanistic learning beyond what they received in their basic schooling.

Those going to college exclusively to advance their general education should seek institutions that offer college programs devised to satisfy this purpose. Too few such institutions now exist; they constitute the exception rather than the rule. We need more college programs in which the major course of study offered is common to all, with but few if any electives permitted. Such colleges would be ideal institutions for the preparation of the teachers to staff our reformed basic schools.

To overcome the specialization that now abounds on all sides, it may be necessary for our graduate and professional schools, at the university level, to leaven the intensity of the specialization they demand by carrying general learning forward at still higher levels.

That our technologically advanced industrial society needs technically trained specialists is beyond question. Intense specialization is always necessary for the advancement of learning in all the learned professions, and in diverse fields of science and scholarship. We cannot turn our backs on these essential needs. Nor can we return to an earlier epoch when such intense specialization was not needed.

But we can and should do something to mitigate the barbarism of intense specialization, which threatens to be as destructive in its own way as the abandonment of specialization would be. We can reconceive the role and offerings of our colleges and universities, made possible by the time saved and the skills acquired that reformed basic schooling will provide.

We need specialists for our economic prosperity, for our national welfare and security, for continued progress in all the arts and sciences, and in all fields of scholarship. But for the sake of our cultural traditions, our democratic institutions, and our individual well-being, our specialists must also be generalists; that is, generally educated human beings.

# 11
# Earning a Living and Living Well

Our main concern is basic schooling. It is the only schooling that is compulsory for all and that should be the same for all.

Our concern is double-edged. We have two fundamental goals in view. One is equipping all the children of this country to earn a good living for themselves. The other is enabling them to lead good human lives.

The enjoyment of a high standard of living, however desirable, still leaves more to be desired. The external, physical, material conditions of a good human life, necessary as they are, remain by themselves insufficient. They must be put to such use by the individual that the quality of his or her life is enriched internally as well as externally.

To raise the standard of living for all, we need—*for all*—a more effective basic schooling than now exists. To improve the quality of life for all, we need—*for all*—a better quality of schooling than now exists.

As compared with the human condition in other countries, most Americans are better off, more have access to the comforts and conveniences of life, more enjoy the material advantages that are indispensable factors in the pursuit of happiness. This aim, the Declaration of Independence boldly asserted, belongs by right to all. As Abraham Lincoln pointed out, that was a pledge to the future; it still remains to be fulfilled.

When we hold before us the equally important results that our proposed reform of basic schooling aims at—earning a better living and enjoying a better quality of life— we are brought face to face with two obstacles that must be overcome. Even if all the others were surmounted, two things would still stand in the way of achieving the needed reform.

One is the uncertain economic status of a substantial part of the school population. The other is the understandable but nevertheless one-sided emphasis that too many parents place on economic and material advantages in thinking of their children's futures.

A basic human right is the right to obtain a decent livelihood by working for it under decent conditions. Those whom the economy leaves unemployed through no fault of their own are unjustly deprived of an essential human right which is indispensable to their pursuit of happiness.

As things stand now, that part of the school population which comes from severely disadvantaged minorities can look forward to unemployment after leaving school— thrown on the waste heap of a society that is squandering its human resources. Hopelessness about the future is bound to affect motivation in school. Why do the hard work that good basic schooling would demand if, after doing it, no opportunity exists to work for a decent living? This bleak prospect makes for the dropout, or, what is just as bad, turns the energetic into the delinquent. While still in school, they regard themselves as prisoners serving time.

The other face of the picture is the attitude of parents who regard all schooling as having no purpose beyond helping graduates to earn a living and get ahead materially.

The truth, hidden from too many, is that more than money and material advantages are necessary for the good life. Children should be prepared and motivated to make themselves the best human beings they are capable of becoming. If a better quality of schooling for all enables them to make a better use of their talents, their energies, their free time, it will also help to improve the quality of life for all.

Two things, then, must go hand in hand with the recommended reform of basic schooling. One is the commitment of our society to a policy of full employment, securing for everyone his or her right to earn a living. The other is the enlightenment of parents with regard to the goals of basic schooling—not just earning a living, but living well.

To put it another way, the monumental effort it will take to improve the quality of basic schooling cannot be justified solely by reference to economic and material advantages. It needs to be undertaken to improve the quality of human life for all.

# 12
# The Future of Our Free Institutions

THE THRUST OF OUR ARGUMENT so far has been that basic schooling ought to prepare every child to earn a living and live a good life. But there is one more reason for exerting every effort to improve basic schooling. We must also do it to preserve our free institutions.

Democratic government and the institutions of a free society are of very recent advent in the world. They are as recent as the enactment of truly universal suffrage and the effort to secure the human and civil rights of the whole population. These are gains made in the twentieth century and not before, made only in a few places on this planet, not everywhere.

What occurred in a few countries for the first time in the twentieth century brought into existence only the initial conditions of a democratic society. It remains to be seen whether these conditions will be preserved and put to good use—whether their promises for the future will be fulfilled.

Both depend in large part on our being able to succeed in improving education in the broadest sense—to produce an educated electorate. As we know, achieving this result presupposes better basic schooling for all, as well as better advanced schooling for some.

You may be apathetic about improving your own life. You may be relatively hopeless about seeing the promises of democracy reach their full fruition. But you cannot love your children and at the same time be callous about the betterment of their lives, together with the betterment of the society in which they will live as adults.

You may be skeptical about the efficacy of your own involvement in political affairs. But you cannot love your country and at the same time be indifferent about the future of its free institutions.

Dismiss these concerns and you have little or no reason to feel a passionate commitment to reforms that will improve the quality of the schooling we give the children of this country.

Harbor no aspirations for the fulfillment of democracy's promises or the enhancement of the lives of its citizens, and you can shrug away the sorry state of our schools today.

But there cannot be more than a few among us who do not have to some degree these passions and these aspirations. The rest of us are deeply moved by them and thus cannot help being aroused to demand for all the children of this nation better schooling than any now available to the vast majority of them. Only a handful, a favored few, now have access to schooling of the quality that all deserve.

Our country faces many insistently urgent problems, on the solution of which its prosperity and even its survival depend—the threat of nuclear war, the shrinking of essential resources and supplies of energy, the pollution or spoliation of the environment, the spiraling of inflation accompanied by the spread of unemployment.

To solve these problems, we need resourceful and innovative leadership. For that to arise and be effective, we must have an educated people. Trained intelligence, in followers as well as in leaders, holds the key to the solution of the problems we face.

Achieving peace, prosperity, and plenty could put this country on the edge of becoming an earthly paradise, but only a much better educational system than now exists can carry us across the threshold.

Without it, a poorly schooled population will not be able to put to good use the opportunities afforded by the achievement of the general welfare. Those who are not schooled to enjoy the blessings of a good society can only despoil its institutions and corrupt themselves.

Human resources are the nation's greatest potential riches. To squander them is to impoverish our future.

# To School Boards and School Administrators:

YOU ASK: *What should we do next Monday morning to get started on the Paideia reform of basic schooling?*

WE ANSWER:

1. *Be sure that in every school—from grade one to grade twelve—there are the three kinds of learning and the three kinds of teaching represented by the Three Columns and see that they interact with one another.*

2. *In all Three Columns—the acquirement of organized knowledge, the development of intellectual skills (skills of learning), and the enlargement of the understanding of basic ideas and values—set standards of accomplishment that challenge both students and teachers to fulfill the high expectations you have for them.*

3. *Eliminate all the nonessentials from the school day, or, if retained, make them extracurricular activities.*

4. *Eliminate from the curriculum all training for specific jobs.*

5. *Introduce the study of a second language for a sufficient period of time to assure competence in its use.*

81

6. *Eliminate all electives from the course of study except the choice of the second language to be studied.*

7. *Use as much as possible of the school day's time for learning and teaching.*

8. *Restore homework, and home projects in the arts and sciences, in increasing amounts from grade one to grade twelve.*

9. *Devise, in your community, appropriate ways of ensuring adequate preschool preparation for those who need it.*

10. *Institute remedial instruction (in the Paideia sense of that term) for those who need it, either individually or in very small groups.*

*Do these ten things in a manner that suits the population of your school, both teachers and students; do these things by making your own choice of the materials to be used and your own organization of the course of study from grade to grade; do them with the three fundamental objectives of basic schooling always in mind, and you will have started on its way the reform of basic schooling upon which the prosperity of this country and the happiness of its citizens depends.*

# Epilogue by a School Administrator

THE PAIDEIA PROPOSAL *is truly an educational manifesto. It is both philosophical and practical, at once sound in theory and workable in fact.*

*This proposal could well be entitled "The Reform of Our Public Schools," for it addresses all the critical areas of concern about our school system.*

*—Teaching children to think, and to use their minds in all forms of learning, is the pervasive concept.*

*—Underscoring the belief that all children are educable, it affirms the right of all children in a democracy to equal educational opportunity—the opportunity to become educated human beings.*

*—Recognizing the importance of the preschool years, it stresses the necessity of early tutelage to provide the nurturing so essential as preparation for formal schooling.*

*—Differentiating between three basic kinds of learning and of instruction, it draws our attention to the need for a clearly defined and carefully structured*

83

*curriculum. All educators can benefit from the reminder that the mind can be improved by*

> *acquisition of information and knowledge*
> *development of intellectual skills*
> *increase of understanding and insight.*

*—The role of the teacher is the key to the entire reform, and an acknowledgment of the necessary development and continuous education of the teacher reflects the prominence of the teacher in the learning process.*

*—Principals with power and knowledge corroborate other research that places the responsibility for good schools in the hands of good educational leaders.*

*Without a doubt, the recommendations presented in this book give hope and guidance for all educators interested in progress. Following this road map, so aptly designed, will help them to cure the many maladies of our beleaguered public schools.*

*It is often true that "there is nothing more difficult to carry out, more perilous to conduct, or more uncertain of success than to initiate a new order of things." A new order is what is called for. The* Paideia Proposal *provides public education in this country with both a challenge and an opportunity!*

RUTH B. LOVE
*General Superintendent of Schools*
*Chicago Board of Education*